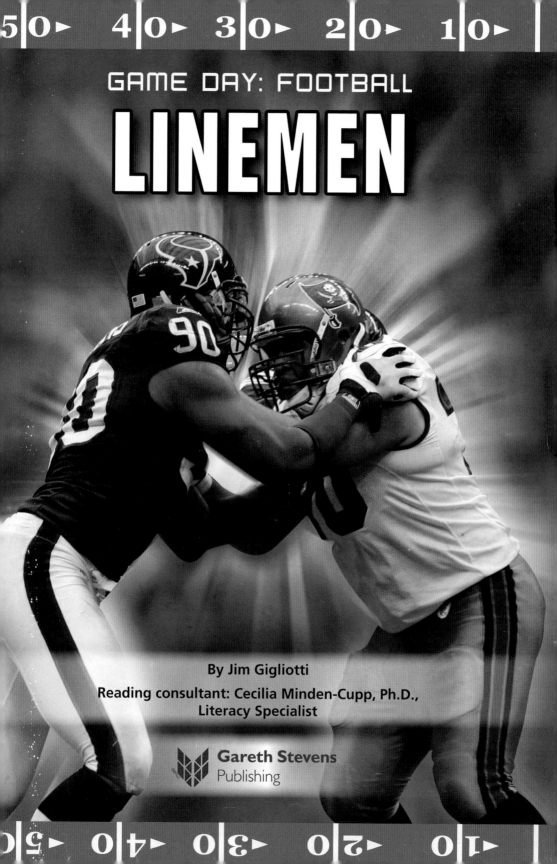

GAME DAY: FOOTBALL

LINEMEN

By Jim Gigliotti

Reading consultant: Cecilia Minden-Cupp, Ph.D.,
Literacy Specialist

Gareth Stevens
Publishing

Please visit our web site at www.garethstevens.com.
For a free catalog describing Gareth Stevens Publishing's list of high-quality books, call 1-800-542-2595 (USA) or 1-800-387-3178 (Canada). Gareth Stevens Publishing's fax: 1-877-542-2596

Library of Congress Cataloging-in-Publication Data
Gigliotti, Jim.
    Linemen / by Jim Gigliotti.
      p. cm. — (Game day. Football)
        Includes bibliographical references and index.
      ISBN-10: 1-4339-1960-5 — ISBN-13: 978-1-4339-1960-2 (lib. bdg.)
      1. Football—Offense—Juvenile literature.   2. Football—Defense—Juvenile literature.
      3. Line play (Football) —Juvenile literature. 4. Football players—United States—
    GV951.2.G55   2010
    796.332'23—dc22   2009002272

This edition first published in 2010 by
Gareth Stevens Publishing
A Weekly Reader® Company
1 Reader's Digest Road
Pleasantville, NY 10570-7000 USA

Copyright © 2010 by Gareth Stevens, Inc.

Executive Managing Editor: Lisa M. Herrington
Senior Editor: Brian Fitzgerald
Senior Designer: Keith Plechaty

Produced by Q2AMedia
Art Direction: Rahul Dhiman
Senior Designer: Dibakar Acharjee
Image Researcher: Kamal Kumar

Photo credits
Key: t = top, b = bottom, c = center, l = left, r = right
Cover and title page: Thomas B. Shea/Getty Images.
Tom Hauck/Getty Images: 4; Donald Miralle/Getty Images: 5; NFL/Getty Images: 6; John Florea/Time & Life Pictures/Getty Images: 7; Twig/NYCSportsPics: 8; Greg Trott/Getty Images: 9; Pro Football Hall of Fame/NFL/Getty Photos/Getty Images: 10; NFL Photos/Getty Images: 11; Rob Tringali/Sportschrome/Getty Images: 12; Kevin Terrell/Getty Images: 13r; Paul Spinelli/Getty Images: 14; G. Newman Lowrance/Getty Images: 15; Gregory Shamus/Getty Images: 16; Joe Robbins/Getty Images: 17; David Stluka/Getty Images: 18; Greg Trott/Getty Images: 19; Bruce Bennett Studios/Getty Images: 20; James Flores/NFL/Getty Images: 21; Ron Vesely/Getty Images: 22; Nate Fine/NFL/Getty Images: 23; Tom Dahlin/Getty Images: 24; Dilip Vishwanat/Getty Images: 25; Kevin Terrell/Getty Images: 26; Jonathan Daniel/Getty Images: 28; Jeff Gross/Getty Images: 29; Gregory Shamus/Getty Images: 30; Joe Robbins/Getty Images: 31; David Drapkin/Getty Images: 32; David Drapkin/Getty Images: 33; Vic Stein/NFL/Getty Images: 34; Vernon Biever/NFL/Getty Images: 35; Tony Tomsic/Getty Images: 36; Al Messerschmidt/Getty Images: 37; Tom Hauck/Getty Images: 38; Bill Baptist/Getty Images: 39; Mike Eliason: 40, 41, 42, 43; Mitchell Layton/Getty Images: 44; Tony Tomsic/Getty Images: 45.
Q2AMedia Art Bank: 13t, 27

Printed in the United States of America

1 2 3 4 5 6 7 8 9 14 13 12 11 10 09

Cover: Mario Williams of the Houston Texans (90) takes on an opposing offensive lineman. Williams is one of the top defensive linemen in pro football.

Contents

Words in the glossary appear in **bold** type the first time they are used in the text.

Super Battle

Football players who pass, catch, and run the ball get the most attention. But players who battle along the **line of scrimmage** are just as important. They are the linemen.

BEST AGAINST THE BEST

The New England Patriots played the New York Giants in Super Bowl XLII. Most experts did not give the Giants a chance. The Patriots had a great offense and a powerful offensive line. The Giants defensive linemen planned to pressure Patriots quarterback Tom Brady. They wanted to stop him from making big plays. That was New York's only chance of winning.

▼ The Giants defensive linemen (in white) face off against the Patriots offensive linemen (in blue) in Super Bowl XLII.

▲ Giants defensive end Michael Strahan sacks Tom Brady (12) during Super Bowl XXLII.

A GIANT PLAY

The Giants' plan worked. They trailed 7–3 midway through the third quarter. The Patriots were in range for a field goal. On third down, Giants defensive end Michael Strahan burst off the line at the snap. He raced around Patriots tackle Nick Kaczur. He **sacked** Brady for a loss. New England was out of field-goal range. Not getting those three points made a big difference. The Giants went on to win 17–14. By winning the battle on the line, New York won the Super Bowl!

GLOSSARY

line of scrimmage: the imaginary line that divides the offense and the defense before each play

sacked: tackled the quarterback behind the line of scrimmage

5

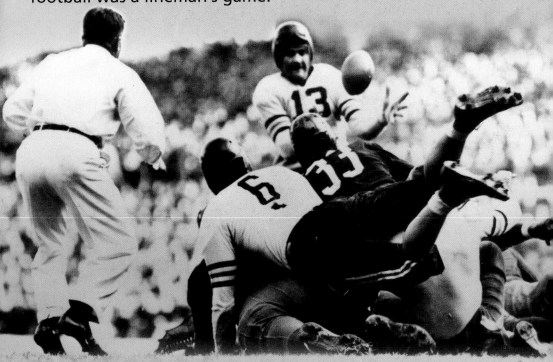

The Rough Old Days

In the early days of football, teams mostly ran the ball. The team that won had the strongest blockers on offense or the strongest tacklers on defense. Early football was a lineman's game.

OFFENSE AND DEFENSE

The National Football League (NFL) was formed in 1920. The rules limited how many substitutes a team could use. New players could come into a game only at certain times. It was the time of the "two-way" player. Players were in the lineup for both offense and defense.

▲ Big pileups at the line of scrimmage were a regular part of early NFL games.

THE GAME CHANGES

In 1943, the NFL began to allow free substitution. Players came into a game and left a game as often as coaches wanted. Passing became more popular. Teams needed offensive linemen who could protect the quarterback on pass plays. They also needed defensive linemen who could rush the passer. The era of the two-way player soon ended.

▼ Linemen watch a receiver catch a pass. As football changed, blockers needed to give the quarterback time to find open receivers.

The Last Two-Way Star

Chuck Bednarik was the last man to play both offense and defense. He played for the Philadelphia Eagles from 1949 to 1962. "Concrete Charlie" was a center on offense. He played linebacker on defense.

WHERE GAMES ARE WON AND LOST

Football has changed a lot since the days of the two-way linemen. Passing is a bigger part of the game. The most successful teams have the best offensive and defensive lines. The "skill" players are the quarterbacks, running backs, and wide receivers. They are the biggest stars. However, the battles on the line determine whether skill players have room to run or time to throw.

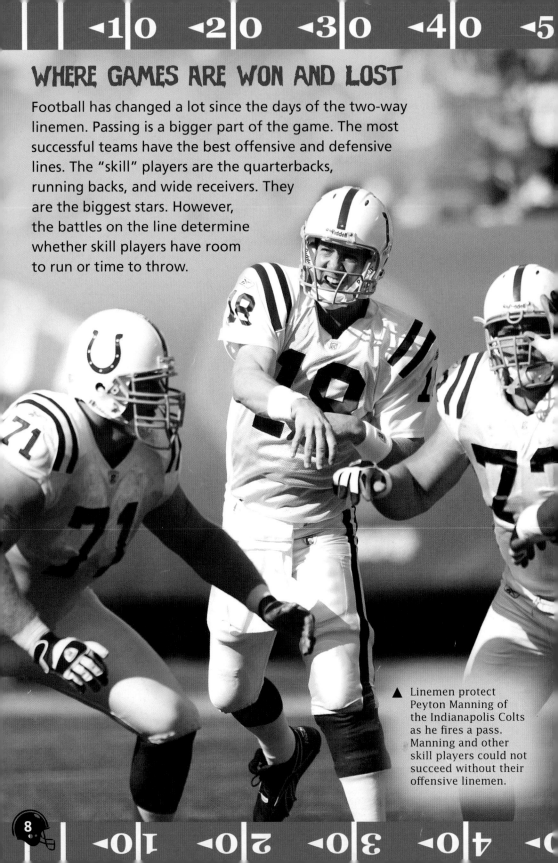

▲ Linemen protect Peyton Manning of the Indianapolis Colts as he fires a pass. Manning and other skill players could not succeed without their offensive linemen.

BIG, BIGGER, BIGGEST

Pete Henry, a 250-pound tackle, played in the NFL in the 1920s. Everyone thought he was huge. Today, Henry would be small for a lineman. Few offensive linemen weigh less than 300 pounds. Most defensive tackles tip the scales at more than 300 pounds, too. Defensive ends weigh a little less.

Fresh Legs

Coaches know that line play makes the difference between winning and losing. Many teams rotate linemen to keep players from tiring out. That is especially true on the defensive line. Rotating players helps them stay strong during the long season.

Offensive linemen spread their feet wide when blocking to give them better balance.

▲ Eagles lineman Max Jean-Gilles (62) weighs 358 pounds. Teammate Jon Runyan (69) is "only" 330 pounds!

The Two-Way Stars

Here are two of the best players from the NFL's two-way era.

SIZE AND SPEED

Cal Hubbard weighed about 250 pounds, but he was fast. He could run the 100-yard dash in 11 seconds. That combination of size and speed made him a force on the offensive and defensive lines. As a **rookie** in 1927, he helped the New York Giants win the NFL title. He joined the Green Bay Packers in 1929. He helped the team win championships in each of his first three seasons.

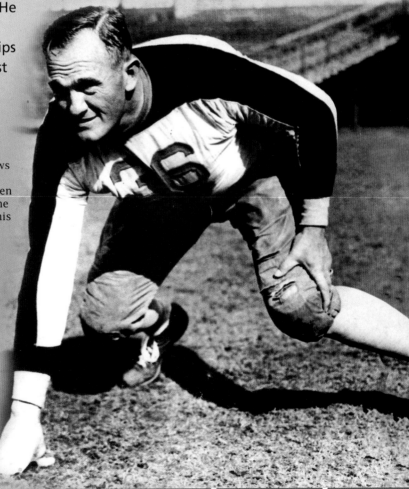

► Cal Hubbard shows the three-point stance that linemen still use today. The three points are his two feet and his right hand.

CENTER OF ATTENTION

Players wore leather helmets without facemasks until the mid-1940s.

Mel Hein joined the New York Giants in 1931. For the next 15 years, he was the team's star center—and linebacker. Hein never missed a game. On offense, he earned all-league honors eight years in a row. On defense, he covered star receivers, such as Green Bay's Don Hutson. In 1938, Hein was named the NFL's Most Valuable Player (MVP).

The center snaps the ball to the quarterback with one hand.

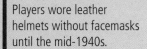

GLOSSARY

rookie: a player in his first season of pro football

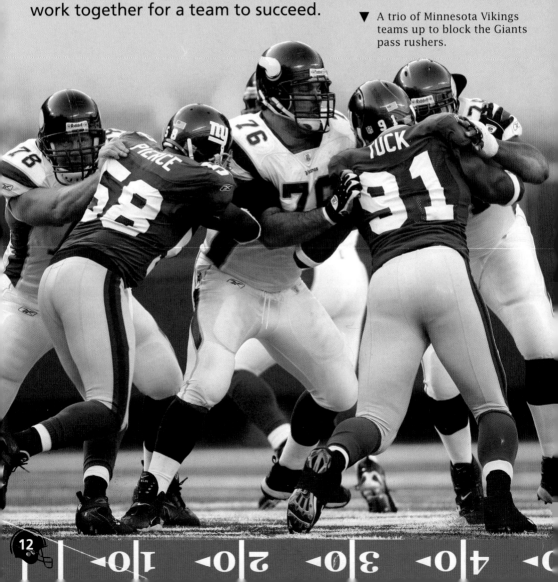

CHAPTER 2

Playing Offensive Line

An offensive lineman doesn't work alone.
He is just one of many parts that must
work together for a team to succeed.

▼ A trio of Minnesota Vikings
teams up to block the Giants
pass rushers.

Key

WR: Wide Receiver	RT: Right Tackle
LT: Left Tackle	TE: Tight End
LG: Left Guard	QB: Quarterback
C: Center	HB: Halfback
RG: Right Guard	FB: Fullback

JOB DESCRIPTIONS

There are five offensive linemen in a standard **formation**. They are the center, two guards, and two tackles. The guards and tackles are also named left or right depending on which side of the line they play.

More Help

The tight end is not considered an offensive lineman. Tight ends usually begin a play on the offensive line. They can also catch passes. Many teams have a tight end who is a blocking specialist. A good blocking tight end is like an extra offensive lineman.

► Quarterback Tony Romo (9) of the Dallas Cowboys awaits the snap from center Andre Gurode. Centers are the only players who are sure to touch the ball on every play.

GLOSSARY

formation: the way that a football team lines up its players on the field

PEOPLE MOVERS

Offensive linemen are often the strongest players on a football team. Sometimes they're called "people movers." They have to shove defensive players around to make room for ball carriers. They are still very athletic. They must have the footwork of a dancer. A 300-pound dancer, that is!

▼ Tackle Walter Jones of the Seattle Seahawks (left) shows excellent blocking technique. He stays low, keeps his head up, and keeps his feet moving.

When blocking, offensive linemen keep their hands out in front of their body.

LOTS TO KNOW

Offensive linemen are among the most intelligent players on a football team. An offensive lineman has to know the job of everyone else on the team. That's one reason offensive linemen can change positions more easily than other players. For instance, if a center is injured, a guard might take over his job. He can do that because he usually knows the job of the center almost as well as his own.

Unwanted Attention

It takes a special type of player to be an offensive lineman. He has to watch other players score all the touchdowns and get all the glory. Often, the only time fans hear an offensive lineman's name is when he commits a penalty!

▼ Members of the Chicago Bears offensive line rest while their defense is on the field. Linemen often meet with coaches on the sidelines.

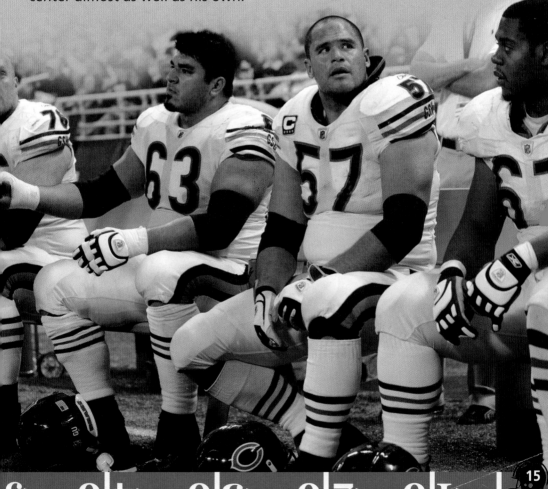

RUN BLOCKING

Offensive linemen block differently for running plays than for passing plays. On running plays, an offensive lineman tries to push the defensive lineman backward. He tries to "knock him off the ball." That creates a **hole** for the ball carrier to run through. The lineman tries to stay between the defender and the ball carrier. He tries to keep the defender from making a tackle.

Not Just for Breakfast

A "pancake" block happens when an offensive lineman knocks a defender off his feet. The defender is flattened, just like a pancake!

▼ Running back Willie Parker of the Pittsburgh Steelers bursts through a hole created by his offensive linemen.

▲ Guard Josh Beekman (67) of the Chicago Bears "pulls" for running back Matt Forte.

TYPES OF BLOCKS

Linemen need to know different types of blocks. A drive block is the most common. That's a straight-ahead block to "drive" the defender backward. On an angle block, the offensive lineman pushes a defender to his left or right. That helps create a hole for a running back. When an offensive lineman "pulls," he leaves his usual position. He then leads a ball carrier up the field.

GLOSSARY

hole: an open area created by blockers into which a ball carrier can run

PASS PROTECTION

Protecting the quarterback is the most important job of an offensive lineman. On passing plays, offensive linemen drop back and form a **pocket** around the passer. The pocket is like a protective shield for the quarterback. The offensive linemen must keep pass rushers from sacking the quarterback. They also must give him enough space to see the field, step, and throw. That's not easy to do when extra pass rushers come on a **blitz!**

The Blind Side

The quarterback can't always see a pass rusher coming from his back side, or blind side. The tackle who protects a quarterback's blind side is very important. For a right-handed quarterback, the blind side is on the left side. For a left-handed quarterback, it is the right side.

▼ Chicago Bears linemen form a pocket of protection around their quarterback.

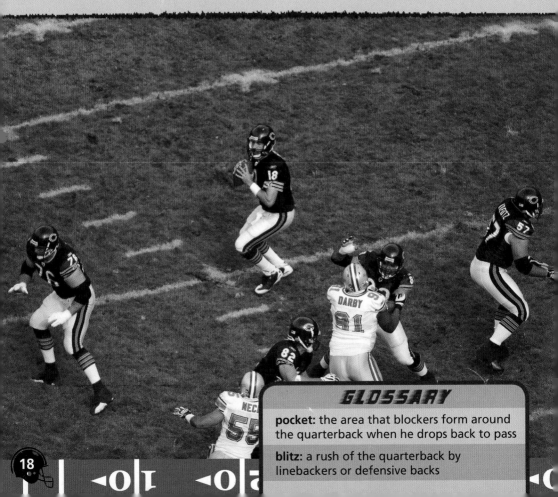

GLOSSARY

pocket: the area that blockers form around the quarterback when he drops back to pass

blitz: a rush of the quarterback by linebackers or defensive backs

ALL FOR ONE AND ONE FOR ALL

Every offensive lineman has to do his job or the play can fail. Bad things can happen if even one of the linemen doesn't do his job. The quarterback might throw an incompletion because he had to throw the ball too soon. The running back might not have room to run. Worse still, the quarterback might be sacked and lose a fumble. That's why offensive line play is so important to the outcome of a game.

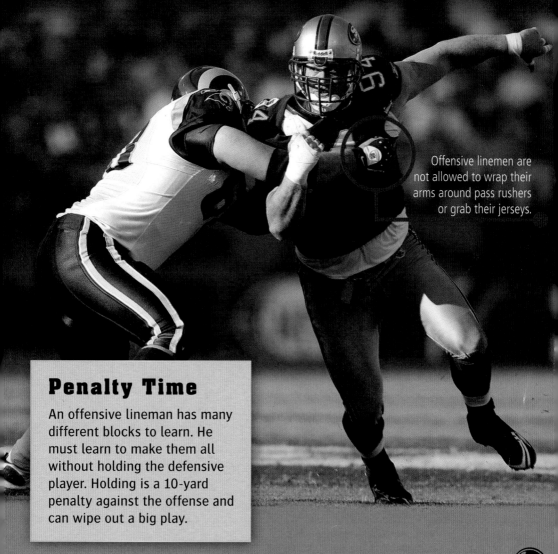

Offensive linemen are not allowed to wrap their arms around pass rushers or grab their jerseys.

Penalty Time

An offensive lineman has many different blocks to learn. He must learn to make them all without holding the defensive player. Holding is a 10-yard penalty against the offense and can wipe out a big play.

CHAPTER

3

Offensive Line Stars

We know what makes a good offensive lineman. Now let's meet some of them! Here are some of the top stars of yesterday and today.

THE FIRST HALL OF FAMER

Jim Parker entered the **Pro Football Hall of Fame** in 1973. He was the first full-time offensive lineman to earn that honor. All linemen before him had been two-way players. Parker starred for the Baltimore Colts for 11 seasons beginning in 1957.

▼ Big Jim Parker (77) spent his career protecting legendary quarterback Johnny Unitas (19).

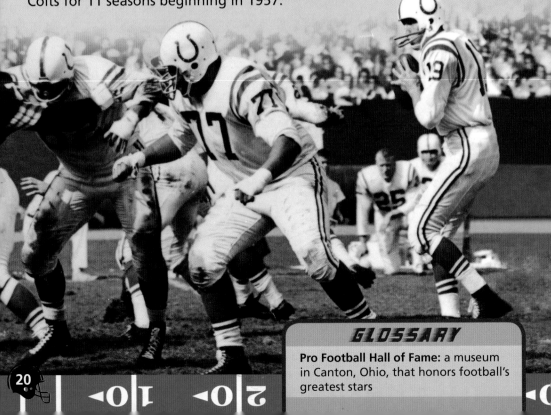

GLOSSARY

Pro Football Hall of Fame: a museum in Canton, Ohio, that honors football's greatest stars

HIGH PRAISE

Legendary coach Vince Lombardi led many great players on the Green Bay Packers teams of the 1960s. He called Forrest Gregg "the finest player I ever coached." Gregg was an all-league tackle for eight seasons beginning in 1960. He played on six Green Bay teams that won NFL titles. He won another one with Dallas.

Double Zero

Center Jim Otto of the Oakland Raiders was an outstanding player at a tough position. He was named to the all-league team 12 times in the 1960s and early 1970s. Otto may have been best known for his unique uniform number: 00.

▲ Forrest Gregg (75, left) takes on the great pass rusher Deacon Jones (75, right).

AWESOME ALL-STAR

Anthony Muñoz played tackle for the Cincinnati Bengals from 1980 to 1992. At 6 feet 6 inches and 278 pounds, he had the strength of an ox. He also had the grace of a ballet dancer. Muñoz did more than mow down defenders. He scored four touchdowns on **tackle-eligible** plays. Muñoz made the **Pro Bowl** 11 times in a row.

PRIDE OF THE PATRIOTS

The Patriots have been the most successful team in the NFL in recent years. That wasn't always the case. The team had been to the playoffs only once before 1973. Then guard John Hannah joined the team. The Patriots built a strong running game around Hannah and became winners. The team had only one losing season in Hannah's last 10 years. In his final season, 1985, the Patriots reached the Super Bowl.

Lots of Jobs

Bruce Matthews was the Houston Oilers top pick in the 1983 **NFL Draft**. He stayed with the club for the next 19 years. (The Oilers became the Tennessee Titans in 1999.) Matthews started games at all five offensive line positions. He was a star wherever he played. He made the Pro Bowl nine times as a center and five times as a guard.

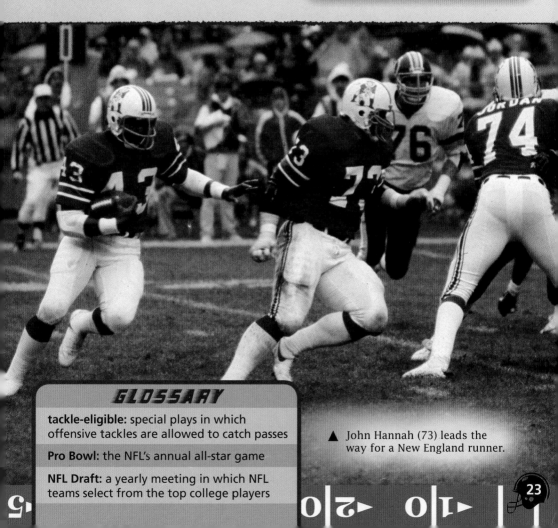

GLOSSARY

tackle-eligible: special plays in which offensive tackles are allowed to catch passes

Pro Bowl: the NFL's annual all-star game

NFL Draft: a yearly meeting in which NFL teams select from the top college players

▲ John Hannah (73) leads the way for a New England runner.

RECORD HELPER

In 2005, Seattle's Shaun Alexander scored an amazing 28 touchdowns. In 2007, Minnesota's Adrian Peterson set an NFL record by rushing for 296 yards in a game. What did those players have in common? They both ran behind guard Steve Hutchinson. He is considered the best in the league at his position. He made the Pro Bowl for the sixth year in a row in 2008.

▶ Steve Hutchinson leads the way for record-setting running back Adrian Peterson.

WHERE IT ALL STARTS

Quarterback Peyton Manning and his talented receivers get most of the attention in Indianapolis. They put up huge offensive numbers. However, every play begins with center Jeff Saturday. He joined the Colts as a rookie guard in 1999. His teammates know that he is one of the keys to their offensive success.

▼ Center Jeff Saturday snaps the ball to quarterback Peyton Manning and immediately begins to block.

CHAPTER 4
Playing Defensive Line

The offensive line does its best to work together. At the same time, the defensive line does everything it can to keep that from happening!

► Linemen Darnell Dockett (90) and Bertrand Berry of the Arizona Cardinals team up for a sack.

BASIC FORMATIONS

Most defensive formations include either three or four linemen. A 3–4 defense has three linemen: two ends and a nose tackle (sometimes called a "nose guard"). The "4" refers to the number of linebackers.

A 4–3 defense has four linemen: two ends and two tackles. They are backed by three linebackers. Most teams today play the 4–3 defense.

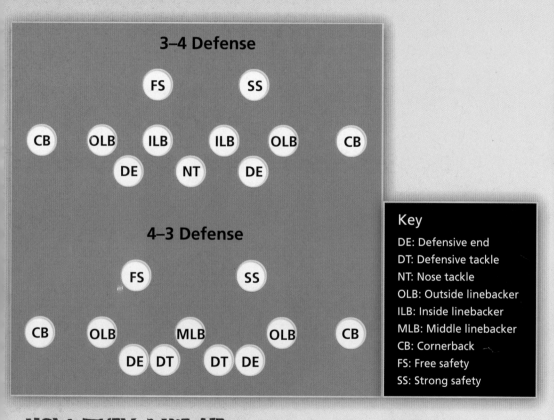

3–4 Defense

FS   SS

CB   OLB   ILB   ILB   OLB   CB

DE   NT   DE

4–3 Defense

FS   SS

CB   OLB   MLB   OLB   CB

DE DT   DT DE

Key

DE: Defensive end
DT: Defensive tackle
NT: Nose tackle
OLB: Outside linebacker
ILB: Inside linebacker
MLB: Middle linebacker
CB: Cornerback
FS: Free safety
SS: Strong safety

HOW THEY LINE UP

In a 4–3 defense, the defensive ends are the main pass rushers. In a 3–4 defense, the outside linebackers are the main pass rushers. On rushing plays, defensive linemen make the tackle when they can. Otherwise, their job is to take on the offensive linemen. That leaves the team's linebackers free to make tackles.

THE RUN STUFFERS

The tackles on the defensive line are called the interior linemen. Their job is to "stuff," or stop, the run. An interior lineman who can also rush the passer is a big bonus.

▼ Big defensive tackle Tommie Harris of the Chicago Bears clogs up the middle of the line. Teams often use two blockers to stop him. That frees up other defenders to make tackles.

THE DEFENSIVE ENDS

▲ Jared Allen of the Minnesota Vikings wraps up Kurt Warner of the Arizona Cardinals for a sack.

The pass-rushing end is the best-known position on a defense. Defensive ends who make a lot of sacks get the most headlines. There's a reason for that. A big sack can turn around a whole game. Sacks mean lost yards for the offense. Sometimes, a sack causes the quarterback to fumble.

MAKING A TACKLE

Defensive linemen—and all football players—need to know how to tackle properly. They must keep their head up to avoid a neck injury. They start low by bending at the knees, not the waist. A lineman is often fighting a blocker—or two—when he tries to make a tackle. He can't always make a picture-perfect stop. Sometimes, he has to just grab on and wait for help.

▲ Defensive end Jay Ratliff (90) of the Dallas Cowboys and a teammate work together to bring down a ball carrier.

► Dwight Freeney (93) of
the Indianapolis Colts
shows why he is one of
the best ends in the NFL.
He keeps going no matter
what the blocker does to
stop him.

LET NOTHING STOP YOU

All defensive linemen need the
right attitude. The run stuffers must
believe that nothing is going to stop
them from getting to the ball carrier.
Pass rushers do whatever it takes to
reach the quarterback. On the line of
scrimmage, it's man on man, strength
against strength!

GET TO THE PASSER!

Defensive linemen need to have a good sense of the game. They must quickly decide whether a play is going to be a run or a pass. They have to be strong enough to overpower bigger offensive linemen. They also have to be quick enough to get to the quarterback before he has time to throw.

▲ Robert Mathis of the Colts strips the ball from an opposing quarterback. Even when pass rushers don't get sacks, they can make life miserable for quarterbacks.

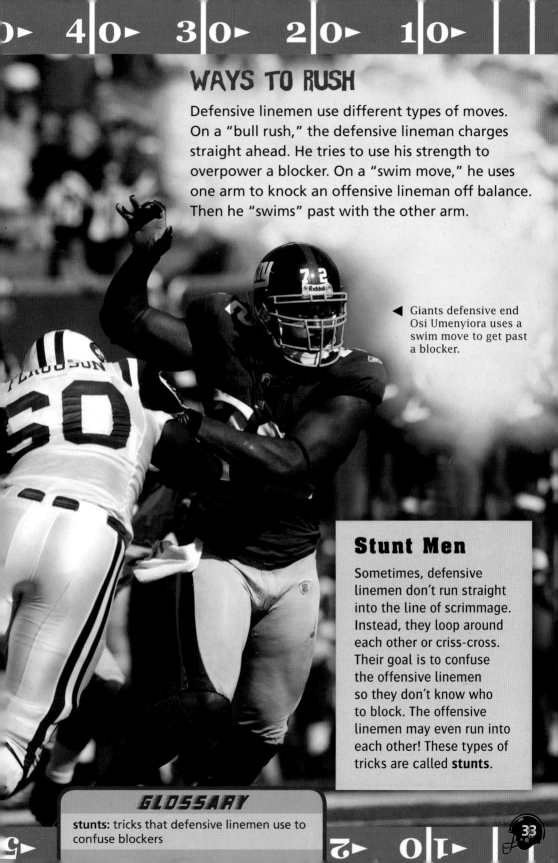

WAYS TO RUSH

Defensive linemen use different types of moves. On a "bull rush," the defensive lineman charges straight ahead. He tries to use his strength to overpower a blocker. On a "swim move," he uses one arm to knock an offensive lineman off balance. Then he "swims" past with the other arm.

◀ Giants defensive end Osi Umenyiora uses a swim move to get past a blocker.

Stunt Men

Sometimes, defensive linemen don't run straight into the line of scrimmage. Instead, they loop around each other or criss-cross. Their goal is to confuse the offensive linemen so they don't know who to block. The offensive linemen may even run into each other! These types of tricks are called **stunts**.

GLOSSARY

stunts: tricks that defensive linemen use to confuse blockers

CHAPTER

5

Defensive Line Stars

Let's meet some of the best defensive linemen—from the 1960s to the present day.

L.A. STORY

Defensive end Deacon Jones of the Los Angeles Rams was a tough pass rusher in the 1960s. He invented the term *sack*. He and his linemates were known as the Fearsome Foursome.

▼ Deacon Jones chases down a New York Giants quarterback. Jones loved nothing more than getting to the football.

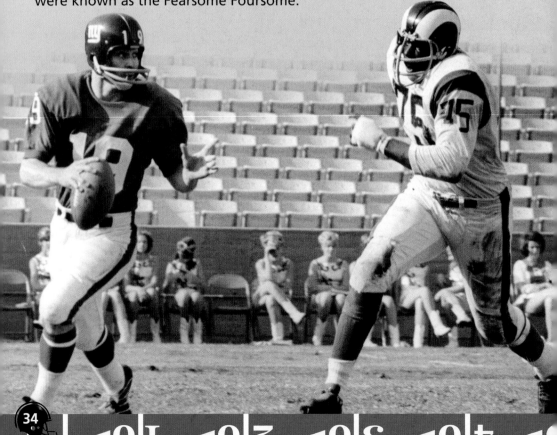

MEAN JOE

Joe Greene's nickname was "Mean Joe." He got the name because his college team was the "Mean Green" of North Texas State. Off the field, Greene was a nice guy. Many NFL offensive linemen, though, thought the nickname fit. For 13 seasons, Greene pushed them around to get to the ball carrier or the opposing quarterback. He helped the Pittsburgh Steelers win four Super Bowls in the 1970s.

◄ Joe Greene was a huge part of "the Steel Curtain" defense in Pittsburgh.

The Name Game

Joe Greene was the star of Pittsburgh's Steel Curtain defense in the 1970s. The Rams had the Fearsome Foursome. Minnesota had a famous defensive line, too: the Purple People Eaters. The Vikings defensive line included future Hall of Famers Carl Eller and Alan Page.

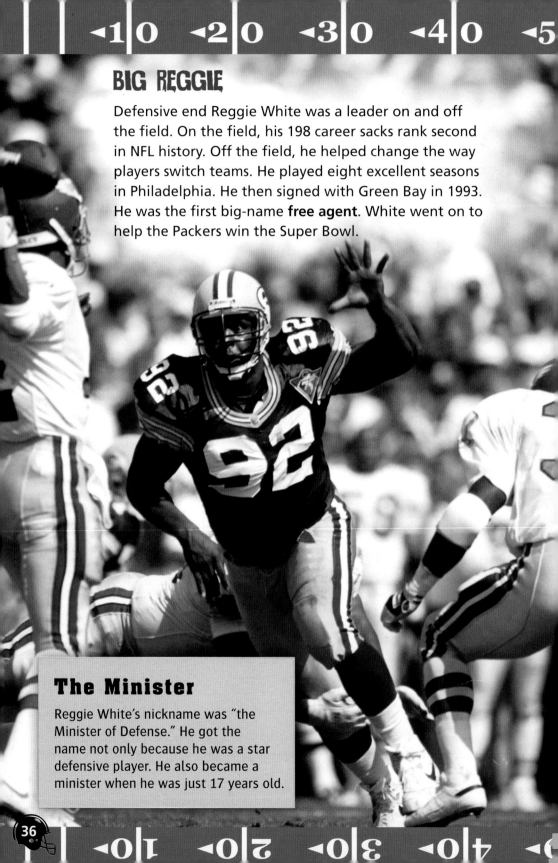

BIG REGGIE

Defensive end Reggie White was a leader on and off the field. On the field, his 198 career sacks rank second in NFL history. Off the field, he helped change the way players switch teams. He played eight excellent seasons in Philadelphia. He then signed with Green Bay in 1993. He was the first big-name **free agent**. White went on to help the Packers win the Super Bowl.

The Minister

Reggie White's nickname was "the Minister of Defense." He got the name not only because he was a star defensive player. He also became a minister when he was just 17 years old.

WALKING AWAY A WINNER

Many athletes talk about going out on top. That's just what New York Giants defensive end Michael Strahan did. He ended a great 15-year career by helping the Giants **upset** the New England Patriots in Super Bowl XLII. His 22.5 sacks in 2001 is the most-ever in a single season.

Half a Sack?

How does a player earn half a sack? He gets half a sack when he joins a teammate in tackling the quarterback behind the line of scrimmage.

▼ Michael Strahan grabs hold of Jake Delhomme of the Carolina Panthers.

GLOSSARY

free agent: a player who has completed his contract with one team and is "free" to sign with any other team

upset: won a game that the team was expected to lose

▲ Julius Peppers uses his speed to track down quarterback Matt Hasselbeck of the Seattle Seahawks.

TWO-SPORT STAR

Julius Peppers of the Carolina Panthers is one of the best athletes in the NFL. His first love was basketball. He played in college for the University of North Carolina. However, Peppers really made a difference on the football field. He is 6 feet 7 inches and 283 pounds. He is strong enough to take on offensive linemen and fast enough to run around them.

HE'S NUMBER ONE

To many experts, star running back Reggie Bush seemed like the obvious choice at the top of the 2006 NFL Draft. But the Houston Texans had another idea. They selected Mario Williams, a defensive end from North Carolina State. Williams has become a Pro Bowl player on a talented young defense for the Texans.

▲ In a matchup of top picks, Mario Williams tackles Reggie Bush for a loss.

CHAPTER

6

Future Star: You!

Want to be a lineman? Here are some good ways to practice important skills.

AT THE SNAP

Offensive linemen need to learn to explode off the line. Set up with other linemen in front of a quarterback. Take your three-point stance. When the quarterback says, "Hike," the center snaps the ball. The other linemen quickly come up into a blocking stance with their elbows at chest level. Practice again and again to improve your reaction time to the snap.

▲ Linemen on both sides of the ball should stay on their toes. Make your steps quick and choppy.

QUICK STARTS

Defensive linemen also need to react quickly. Have the quarterback line up opposite the defensive linemen. The quarterback calls signals. At the snap, the linemen charge forward five yards—not at the quarterback! The quarterback should change the **snap count** each time. That helps defensive linemen keep their eyes on the ball and react to its movement.

Warning!

Don't try tackling until you have the proper safety equipment and are working with a coach. This will keep you and your friends from getting hurt. The football players you see on TV wear a lot of padding to go along with their helmet. They learned the proper way to block and tackle from a coach.

GLOSSARY

snap count: the words or numbers that a quarterback calls out to start each play

HEAD-TO-HEAD

This drill is mainly for defensive linemen. Line up opposite a friend who is the blocker. When the ball is snapped, come up quickly and start to try to push past the blocker. Don't hit or collide! This is just to practice the skill of coming up in a good position to make a play. Try to get your hands high on the blocker. When you're in pads, you'll learn more about how to make moves shown earlier in this book.

KNOCK IT DOWN!

Defensive linemen can cause problems for quarterbacks. To practice rushing the quarterback, have a friend drop back to pass. Then rush at him and try to tag him with two hands. If he starts to throw before you reach him, get your hands up above your head. That makes it hard for a passer to see the receiver. You might even deflect, or knock down, the pass. Don't give up!

Watch and See

Tune in to a football game on television. Pay special attention to the battle along the line of scrimmage. That can be tricky because the camera always follows the ball. Watch how the linemen block for the ball carrier on rushing plays. On passing plays, see how the offensive linemen protect their quarterback. See also how the defensive linemen try to get to the passer.

Record Book

Who are the best of the best? Here are the top five linemen in some key categories.

Sacks, Career
1. Bruce Smith: 200.0
2. Reggie White: 198.0
3. Chris Doleman: 147.0
4. Michael Strahan: 141.5
5. Richard Dent: 137.5
   John Randle: 137.5

Note: Doleman also had 3.5 sacks while playing linebacker.

Sacks, Season
1. Michael Strahan, Giants: 22.5 (2001)
2. Mark Gastineau, Jets: 22.0 (1984)
3. Reggie White, Eagles: 21.0 (1987)
   Chris Doleman, Vikings: 21.0 (1989)
5. Mark Gastineau, Jets: 19.0 (1983)
   Bruce Smith, Bills: 19.0 (1990)
   Clyde Simmons, Eagles: 19.0 (1992)

BRUCE SMITH

* All records are through the 2008 season.

Pro Bowls: Offensive Linemen
1. Bruce Matthews (G–C): 14
2. Jim Otto (C): 12
3. Randall McDaniel (G): 12
4. Will Shields (G): 12
5. Tom Mack, (G): 11
   Anthony Muñoz (T): 11
   William Roaf (T): 11
   Larry Allen (G): 11

Pro Bowls: Defensive Linemen
1. Merlin Olsen (DE): 14
2. Reggie White (DE): 13
3. Bob Lilly (DT): 11
   Gino Marchetti (DE): 11
   Bruce Smith (DE): 11

BRUCE MATTHEWS

Glossary

blitz: a rush of the quarterback by linebackers or defensive backs

formation: the way that a football team lines up its players on the field

free agent: a player who has completed his contract with one team and is "free" to sign with any other team

hole: an open area created by blockers into which a ball carrier can run

line of scrimmage: the imaginary line that divides the offense and the defense before each play

pocket: the area that blockers form around the quarterback when he drops back to pass

Pro Bowl: the NFL's annual all-star game

Pro Football Hall of Fame: a museum in Canton, Ohio, that honors football's greatest stars

NFL Draft: a yearly meeting in which NFL teams select from the top college players

rookie: a player in his first season of pro football

sacked: tackled the quarterback behind the line of scrimmage

snap count: the words or numbers that a quarterback calls out to start each play

stunts: tricks that defensive linemen use to confuse blockers

tackle-eligible: special plays in which offensive tackles are allowed to catch passes

upset: won a game that the team was expected to lose

Find Out More

Books

Buckley, James. Jr. *Eyewitness Football*. New York: DK Publishing, 1999.

Gigliotti, Jim. *LaDainian Tomlinson*. Mankato, MN: Child's World, 2006.

Polzer, Tim. *Play Football!* New York: DK Publishing, 2003.

Stewart, Mark. *The Ultimate 10: Football*. Pleasantville, N.Y.: Gareth Stevens, 2009.

Web Sites

www.nfl.com

The official web site of the National Football League is packed with stats, video, news, and player biographies. Football fans will find all they need to know about their favorite players and teams here.

www.nflrush.com

Check out the official kids' site of the NFL. Meet star players, see video of great plays, and get tips from the pros!

www.profootballhof.com

Find out more about the history of pro football and meet the legends of the game at the Pro Football Hall of Fame site.

Index

About the Author

Jim Gigliotti is a freelance writer who lives in southern California with his wife and two children. A former editor at NFL Publishing, he has written more than two dozen books for youngsters and adults, including *Stadium Stories: USC Trojans* and kids' titles on football stars Tom Brady, Peyton Manning, and LaDainian Tomlinson.